I0478486

8 SECRETS TO MAINTAIN MORE LISTINGS, SATISFY SELLERS, AND CASH MORE COMMISSION CHECKS!

"Perception is Reality"

Anonymous

8 SECRETS TO MAINTAIN MORE LISTINGS, SATISFY SELLERS, AND CASH MORE COMMISSION CHECKS!
A step-by-step guide to retaining more listings…and making more commissions

Contents

"It ain't ignorance causes so much trouble; its folks knowing so much that ain't so."

-Josh Billings

8 SECRETS TO MAINTAIN MORE LISTINGS, SATISFY SELLERS, AND CASH MORE COMMISSION CHECKS!
A step-by-step guide to retaining more listings...and making more commissions!

Seller Complaints

When it comes to real estate sales people and public's perception, we rank just above used car salespeople and attorneys.

Why...?

Because so many people have had bad experiences with real estate salespeople! Most states require some form of licensure to practice real estate...none that I am aware of require a separate license to sell commercial real estate.

The problem is that all licensure programs are designed to *"render the practitioner minimally dangerous"* to the public. Licensure programs **do not** teach the new agent how to practice real estate.

Complaint number one...

"They listed my property and never did anything" It is not enough to list a property, put it in LoopNet or the MLS and hope it sells.

The new market reality is that it takes a campaign to get a buyer to raise their hand! You can't just plant a sign and hope that a buyer magically appears...it's going to take some effort.

The mission is to create a quick easy to follow plan that can be used over and over again to market and promote you listings.

Complaint number two...

"I never heard from them again" I gave them my listing for six months and I never heard from the agent again.

I know, this isn't you...but somewhere out there is an agent that took a listing and then for one reason or another didn't communicate with the seller. It could be that they got busy and forgot about this one or that it simply slipped through the cracks.

The problem is the longer it goes between communications that harder it becomes...it's like calling mother after not having called her for a couple of months!

I say communicate early and often...even if it's to say nothing happened!

Complaint number three...

"I don't think they even advertised my property"

Unless you tell the sellers where you are promoting their property there is little if any chance of them actually finding out about the advertisements. Think about it, if they are busy enough to hire you to market their property chances are they are focused on their core business and not "surfing" the web looking for your offering.

You need to promote the property and get it in front of the most probable audience for the particular asset type being offered.

Secrets of listing retention...

Secret number one...it takes a campaign!

<u>To work in an organized and active way toward a particular goal.</u> rommo

Notice it didn't say to just throw enough crap at the wall and hope some sticks.

You have to begin with the goal in mind...and that goal is to sell the property.

Ideally, we would like to get a number of buyers in a controlled competition for the property that way we can hold the line on both pricing and performance.

cam·paign
/kam'pān/ ◄

noun

1. a series of military operations intended to achieve a particular objective, confined to a particular area, or involving a specified type of fighting.
   "a desert campaign"
   synonyms: military operation(s), maneuver(s); More

verb

1. work in an organized and active way toward a particular goal, typically a political or social one.
   "people who campaigned against child labor"
   synonyms: crusade, fight, battle, push, press, strive, struggle, lobby More

Attached as a bonus is a marketing campaign checklist...listing free or low cost websites where you can promote your listings this is just one small part of your overall campaign.

This checklist along with the bonus listing retention letter will help you keep more listings and actually sell more property.

Secret number two...Plant your flag...sign!

As archaic as it may seem signs do seem to work...sometimes!

Your signs need to be fresh looking and attractive. Beat up old signs or torn banner should never be used unless out of desperation.

You want to get a sign up on the property as soon as possible. Not every owner will agree, in fact some will object citing the argument that they either don't want their tenants, employees, suppliers or neighbors to know.

The seller needs to know that in this the information age sooner or later somebody, somewhere is going to find out…might as well deal with it now.

The best way to minimize the "shock" is to get out ahead of it and let the relevant people know that the property is on the market. They may even have an interest in the property themselves or know somebody who would.

Prepare some extra brochures or flyers and leave them with the seller…who knows someone might walk in and have an interest in the property.

Secret number three…Promote!

Now that of a marketing campaign checklist, each month we scan the internet looking for new free or low cost ways to promote properties for sale.

Some of those include the well-known like LoopNet, CoStar, and CityFeet and others. What a lot of agents miss is there is a tremendous opportunity to promote on lesser known sites that get results. Sites like Craigs List, BackPage, NNNex, Property Shark and many more.

Remember the mission is to provide the seller the broadest possible exposure.

The good news about most of these sites is that they are all pretty much cut and paste so once you have your property description, photos, maps, aerials, site plan, floor plan and whatever else you would like to serve up you just upload and go.

A word to the wise…ads without pictures are worthless! If you put a listing on any of the services without a picture you may have not put it on at all. People, agents, and buyers are visual and if they don't see a picture the first thing they are going to wonder is "what's wrong with the property"

Secret number four…Neighbors!

Think about this for a minute, what do you think the likelihood is that someone who owns a building in that area may be interested in owning another building in that area?

I once sold a warehouse in 23 hours for at least $100,000 more than it was worth…to the guy who owned the building right behind my new listing. Why did he move so quickly and pay more?

He wanted to lock out the competition and ultimately gain control of the entire block.

Think about it, the prospective buyer knows the market. They already know the rental rates and trends in the market. They are intimately familiar with the operating expenses for the area and they know who the best leasing and or property management companies are.

Neighbors make one of the best sources of prospective buyers for your listings. (and sellers too)

The beauty is this gives you at least three opportunities to meet the neighbors as well. You can call or send a just listed letter informing them that the property is available. You could call or mail when the property goes under contract and inform them that you are looking for additional property to satisfy buyers that surfaced as a result of your marketing campaign. When the property has closed you can send a "just closed" card or lob in a follow up call and see if they have any interest in making a change.

Secret number five…Expose yourself!

<u>NO</u>…not like that! Most agents network the wrong way.

Think about it with very rare exceptions is there going to be a fellow agent at the cocktail reception that is going to want to buy your new listing.

I didn't say not to network…just do it smarter!

How about showing up where your target audience is…like the local Manufacturers Association. If you work in industrial real estate and there is a large manufacturing community in your market wouldn't it make sense to be a member of the trade group that represents your target audience?

Or if you specialize in retail you may want to join the local retailers association. Most if not all trades or profession have some sort of trade group that lobbies on behalf of that group.

Look for "gaps" in the market place places that most brokers wouldn't even consider or discover and take any and every opportunity to position yourself as the expert in that field.

Secret number six…organize, strategize, maximize!

Make the process easy…on you!

First, get organized when you are campaigning make sure you have everything you need right at your fingertips. I use a transaction folder in that folder I have several subfolder, financials, photos, maps & aerials, correspondence, documents, agreements, comparables, and brochures and executive summary.

I usually write an executive summary in Word so that I can cut and paste in all the websites that way I don't have to rewrite it every time or remember what I said or may have forgotten in the last ad. I write the executive summary to describe the property how large the lot is, the building, what it's constructed of, any special features, traffic counts etc.

I take all the photos of the property and drop them right in the photos file. I grab an aerial from the property appraiser or Google Earth. If the owner has a survey or floor plan in they go.

Strategize, think about who your target audience is. Is this an owner user building or is it an investment property? Is it for lease or for sale? That may sound like a silly question but the differences between the target market is enormous.

Now that you have an idea who is the proper candidate for the property ask yourself what is important to them. What do they want or need in a property and try to couch everything you produce, flyers, brochures, websites, and advertisements in short everything to help meet those needs or answer their questions.

Maximize, where do the work, live, shop, or sell? Earlier I mentioned trade associations any number of different vocations find them and get into the meetings or luncheons. The local chamber of commerce can be a great place to find clients. Don't just go to a chamber meeting and expect to get leads, it may happen but probably not that often. Instead get on the Ambassadors committee, Ambassadors go out and great all the new and existing business owners and members usually to deliver a plaque or emblem.

Secret number seven…Memorialize!

Now that you have all these different marketing opportunities working for you make sure you track and keep track of everything. Keep you checklist handy in fact I keep it in the front of my paper…yes, paper listing folder.

I am more than a little paranoid but, my manila folder has never crashed, gotten a virus, failed to connect to the internet or been stolen (once it was thrown out by mistake). Paper files are a bit cumbersome in that they do take up room and you have to haul them around but they are always at hand when you need them.

Also, if you ever have an occasion to have a seller try to give you a fee-haircut because you "didn't work that hard" to make that huge commission you can whip out the entire "paper trail" copy of ads, correspondence and _viola_…problem solved!

Secret number eight…

Toot your own horn…no one else is going to do it for you!

Remember when we started this conversation…it was all about retaining listings and satisfying more sellers and cashing more commission checks well here comes the punch line.

First, remember what your objective is…for this discussion we are talking about the actions that will help you retain more listings. By servicing the seller and providing weekly updates you will prove the faith and confidence that seller entrusted you with was fully justified.

If you follow the steps in the marketing plan and marketing campaign checklist you will be doing one new marketing activity each week. Now it doesn't matter if you are ambitious and get them all done over the weekend or you actually do them once a week the objective is to provide a copy of the ad or flyer along with a personalized copy of the matching letter.

Perception is reality. If the seller is getting your weekly written updates the seller will believe that you are actively marketing his or her property. And guess what you are…you are now doing hundreds of times more work than your nearest competitor.

Send the seller a copy of your latest ad or flyer last thing Friday that way they get it first thing Monday or Tuesday and they can spend the entire week ruminating on all the efforts you are making on their behalf.

Do not…**DO NOT** rely on someone else to do this for you unless it is your paid assistant. It is up to you to make sure that it happens and if you ever lose a listing because you didn't keep the seller apprised you only have to look in the mirror to find who to blame.

I like to send a letter to the seller every time I show the property that way I can prove I am working for them and I can register the prospective buyer in case we part company and that buyer would reappear on the scene.

I will even send the seller a letter to tell them that nothing happened…for example I might send a letter that says it's the holiday week and as usual nothing happens but after the holiday (Christmas, New Years, Yom Kippur, Kwanza) we expect to start seeing some interest again.

Lastly, while you're out doing all this marketing something completely unexpected may happen, you may actually find a buyer for the property and close it.

COMMERCIAL INVESTMENT
REAL ESTATE ACADEMY

Sunday, May 21, 2017

Mr. _____

_____

_____

Re: *XYZ Realty* Exclusive Marketing Plan

Dear _____,

I just wanted to take a minute to thank you for your commitment to *XYZ Realty* in the marketing your property.

A successful outcome for you is our number one concern. We will strive to keep your property in the front of the greatest number of qualified buyers possible. In addition to that while we are bound to present *"any and all reasonable offers"* you remain fully in the driver's seat.

We will work diligently to make sure that only truly qualified buyers are shown your property, and that we *"vet"* to the best of our ability their ability to close in a timely fashion, at a price that maximizes your return.

As always, our objective is to put buyers in a *"controlled competition"* for your asset, that way we not only hold the line on price but more importantly on performance. From time to time we will be providing you copies of promotional materials, registrations, and the names of parties that have inquired so you know exactly what we are doing on your behalf.

Thank you again for the opportunity to serve.

COMMERCIAL INVESTMENT
REAL ESTATE ACADEMY

Tuesday, October 23, 2012

Mr. _____

_____

_____

_____

Re: Catylist Posting

Dear _____,

Attached you will please find a copy of our Catylist Cmail marketing flyer according to Catylist *"Catylist is the #1 provider of CIE software, serving REALTOR® associations in over 30 local and regional markets throughout the United States — more than any other provider. There are three things that put us head-and-shoulders above other providers: our unique Model, leading Technology, and exceptional Customer Service"*

There are over 30,000 hits per month on Catylist by brokers looking for that special property for their clients. As a major part of the service Catylist sends out thousands of email pushes each and every month to its members of featured properties.

This is just another way we strive to keep your property on the top of the pile and in front of the most active and likely buyers.

Thank you again for your confidence and commitment.

COMMERCIAL INVESTMENT
REAL ESTATE ACADEMY

Tuesday, October 23, 2012

Mr. _____

_____

_____

_____

Re: Craig's List internet posting

Dear _____,

Craig's List is a general marketing site that resembles Backpage and any number of other general marketing sites, however by using "*spaced repetition*" in placing the ad's we keep the posting fresh and at the top of the pile.

While Craig's List may seem like an non-traditional way to market a property the name of the game is exposure and the more "hits" we can generate the more likely it is that we can find the right buyer at the right time.

Craig's List is just another one of the tools that we use to keep your property on the top of the pile and in front of the most active and likely buyers.

Thank you again for your confidence and commitment.

COMMERCIAL INVESTMENT
REAL ESTATE ACADEMY

Tuesday, October 23, 2012

Mr. _____
_____
_____
_____

Re: Buildingsearch.com posting

Dear _____,

Buildingsearch.com is a general marketing site that resembles LoopNet and CoStar and touts itself as follows:

"BuildingSearch is one of the fastest growing application service providers for the commercial real estate industry. We work to aggregate available office, retail, industrial, and land listings across the United States and to create useful applications to help our users exchange information and business requirements as efficiently as possible. Approximately 115,000 people have registered to use BuildingSearch.com. By 2015 we expect to have 500,000 people using BuildingSearch.com to source available property, to market listings, and to use our growing set of commercial real estate applications and services."

By using technology like Buildingsearch.com as part of our multi-faceted approach we continue to expose your property to the widest, most diverse possible audience in our ongoing effort to get you the best possible price and terms.

Thank you for your ongoing business.

COMMERCIAL INVESTMENT
REAL ESTATE ACADEMY

Tuesday, October 23, 2012

Mr. _____

_____

_____

_____

Re: Florida Commercial Information Exchange (FlaCIE)

Dear _____,

Florida Commercial Information Exchange is a sophisticated commercial only, web portal that allows us to quickly and easily present your property to all the commercial practitioners in the Tri-county market area.

By placing your property on FlaCie you property is instantly available to nearly 10,000 commercial real estate practitioners complete with pictures, maps, aerials and the requisite financial data.

It is not at all uncommon for one or more of these commercial brokers to have at least one buyer involved in a IRS Section 1031 Tax Deferred Exchange, these are ideal buyers because they have to buy! Under the rule they have 45 days to identify a *"replacement"* property and an additional 180 days to close. If they fail they <u>pay the taxes</u>…so they are motivated.

Again, this is just another method that we use to identify a probable, motivated buyer.

Thank you for your ongoing business.

COMMERCIAL INVESTMENT
REAL ESTATE ACADEMY

Tuesday, October 23, 2012

Mr. _____

_____

_____

_____

Re: Elistit.com marketing and web posting

Dear _____,

This week we posted your property on Elistit.com, Elistit.com is a real estate web portal that covers both commercial and residential real estate and is sponsored by a major residential real estate company.

The benefit is that most if not all national residential companies do not allow their residential agents to transact commercial transaction, so they have to rely on a commercial practitioner to transact a sale for them.

Many residential owners are business owners and or investors and they look to their relationships to source transections for them. It is not unheard of for a residential agent to *"trip"* over a commercial buyer in the process of selling them a home.

By getting as many eyes on the case a possible we have a greater chance of finding that perfect buyer for your property, this is just another strategy we employ to help get your property maximum exposure.

Thank you for your continued commitment and confidence.

COMMERCIAL INVESTMENT
REAL ESTATE ACADEMY

Tuesday, October 23, 2012

Mr. _____
_____
_____
_____

Re: E-propertylinks.com and web posting

Dear _____,

This week we posted your property on E-proeprtylinks.com, E-propertylinks.com is a real estate web portal that covers both commercial and to a lesser extent, residential real estate and is sponsored by a nearly 30 different sponsoring companies.

Originally, E-propertylinks.com originally started with nearly 17,500 members in 2007 and has grown exponentially since then. E-propertylinks.com maintains a list 1.46 million emails and has maintains monthly contact with those professionals.

E-proeprtylists.com routinely broadcasts new listing and has a property search/match service where investors can put in their preferences and get properties flagged for them based on those requirements.

We use E-propertylists.com as one of the numerous tools available to create a marketing "*buzz*" around your property. All in an effort to get buyers into a competition for your property.

Thank you for your continued commitment and confidence.

COMMERCIAL INVESTMENT
REAL ESTATE ACADEMY

Sunday, May 21, 2017

Mr. _____

_____

_____

_____

Re: RealBuyer-Recyber Net Work broadcast email

Dear _____,

This week we broadcast emailed your property to approximately Thirty (30) prospective buyers, these buyers came from an *"opt-in"* service called RealBuyer-Recyber Network.

According to RealBuyer; *"RealBuyer Direct is a searchable national database of over 7000 institutional and investment property buyers and tenants including their detailed investment criteria and contact information. Simply enter the criteria for the buyer, seller or tenant you wish to reach. You may also do a separate search by company name."*

Remember, these are *"opt-in"* prospects not an email scrape of somebody else's list these are real estate buyer that have looked at the site and its services and have chosen to get emails regarding new property offerings.

We constantly strive to use the latest and hopefully the greatest sources available to quickly and efficiently get you property exposed to the maximum number of prospective buyers in the least amount of time.

Thank you for the ongoing opportunity to continue to serve you.

COMMERCIAL INVESTMENT
REAL ESTATE ACADEMY

Monday March 24, 2014

Mr. _____

_____

_____

_____

Re: CoStar real estate website and broadcast services

Gentlemen,

This week we submitted your property to CoStar the Global leader in commercial real estate listing and marketing services. CoStar maintains the largest database of property for sale and lease in the world as you can see below.

"Founded in 1987, CoStar conducts expansive, ongoing research to produce and maintain the largest and most comprehensive database of commercial real estate information. Our suite of online services enables clients to analyze, interpret and gain unmatched insight on commercial property values, market conditions and current availabilities.

Headquartered in Washington, DC, CoStar maintains offices throughout the U.S. and in Europe with a staff of approximately 1,500 worldwide, including the industry's largest professional research organization."

CoStar logs over 5.1 million data changes each day, and logs over 10,000 calls daily to brokers, developers, and other commercial professionals. They currently track 500,000 properties in the US annually and are a go to source for many investors and owners.

Thank you for the ongoing opportunity to continue to serve you.

COMMERCIAL INVESTMENT
REAL ESTATE ACADEMY

Tuesday, October 23, 2012

Mr. _____

_____

_____

_____

Re: Site To Do Business, CCIMRedex

Dear _____,

The Site To Do Business is a proprietary site for Certified Commercial Investment Members, or CCIM's, the CCIM designation is offered by and through the Investment Real Estate Institute a division of the National Association of Realtors.

"A CCIM is part of a global commercial real estate network with members across North America and more than 30 countries. This professional network has enabled CCIM members to close thousands of transactions annually, representing more than $200 billion in value. As a result, the experts who possess the CCIM designation are an invaluable resource for commercial real estate owners, investors, and users."

"Over 15,000 commercial real estate professionals have earned the designation. Currently, 5,500 professionals are pursuing their CCIM designation."

The chances are good that one or more of those real estate professionals is looking for a property just like yours, and we know that we are dealing with a seasoned professional.

Thank you for the ongoing opportunity to continue to serve you.

COMMERCIAL INVESTMENT
REAL ESTATE ACADEMY

Sunday, May 21, 2017

Mr. _____
_____
_____
_____

Re: Weekly Internal Sales Meeting

Dear _____,

Today we had our weekly internal sales meeting, your property (_____) was presented to the agents in attendance including our Broker _____.

It is not at all uncommon for an agent in the office to have a prospective Buyer that is either looking to change product types or is involved in a 1031 Tax Deferred Exchange and looking for a replacement property.

The idea is to keep your property at the "Top of the pile" to help maximize the exposure and get the broadest possible spectrum of Buyers interested in your offering.

Again, this is just one of the many ways we will continue to promote your property on an ongoing basis.

Thank you again for your confidence and commitment.

COMMERCIAL INVESTMENT
REAL ESTATE ACADEMY

Tuesday, October 23, 2012

Mr. _____

_____

_____

_____

Re: Property Blast E-Blast

Dear _____,

This week we blasted you property to over 90,000 commercial real estate brokers nationwide using Property Campaign. Property Campaign is an email push service that is strictly "opt-in" meaning all the brokers and professionals have signed up to get property emailed to them for consideration

Property Campaign is a "*power tool*" for reaching the most aggressive and active brokers in the market place. The objective is getting your asset in front of as many active commercial investment professionals as quickly as possible we hope to create an "*auction like atmosphere*" around your property.

That way we can hold the line on price, but more importantly we can hold the line on performance, after all anyone can write you a contract for anything but if it fails to close what did it matter?

This is just another example of how we strive to help you obtain the best possible price and terms for your real property.

Thank you for the opportunity to serve you.

COMMERCIAL INVESTMENT
REAL ESTATE ACADEMY

May 21, 2017

Mr. _____

_____

_____

_____

Re: Property Line

Dear _____,

This week we blasted your property to over 90,000 commercial real estate brokers nationwide using Property Line. Property Campaign is an email push service that is strictly "opt-in" meaning all the brokers and professionals have signed up to get property emailed to them for consideration

Property Campaign is a "*power tool*" for reaching the most aggressive and active brokers in the market place. The objective is getting your asset in front of as many active commercial investment professionals as quickly as possible we hope to create an "*auction like atmosphere*" around your property.

That way we can hold the line on price, but more importantly we can hold the line on performance, after all anyone can write you a contract for anything but if it fails to close what did it matter?

This is just another example of how we strive to help you obtain the best possible price and terms for your real property.

Thank you for the opportunity to serve you.

Sincerely,

Tuesday, October 23, 2012

Mr. _____
_____
_____
_____

Re: Mondinion Website

Dear _____,

This week we posted your property on Mondinion, Mondinion is an International website that features both commercial residential properties world wide.

According to Mondinion; "*The aim of Mondinion.com is to become the number 1 destination for international real estate, a real estate portal where investors and home buyers meet real estate agents, developers and home owners. For agents and home owners, we provide an easy way to list all their properties for free while investors can use our comprehensive search function to locate the properties of their dreams.*"

Mondinion features over 119,116 active listings at the time of this letter.

Remember, these are "*opt-in*" prospects not an email scrape of somebody else's list these are real estate buyer that have looked at the site and its services and have chosen to get emails regarding new property offerings.

We constantly strive to use the latest and hopefully the greatest sources available to quickly and efficiently get you property exposed to the maximum number of prospective buyers in the least amount of time.

Thank you for the ongoing opportunity to continue to serve you.

COMMERCIAL INVESTMENT
REAL ESTATE ACADEMY

May 21, 2017

Mr. _____

_____

_____

_____

Re: Marketedge Campaign

Dear _____,

This week we sent your property to commercial real estate brokers nationwide using a Marketedgep property Campaign. Marketedge is an listing/email service that is strictly "opt-in" meaning all the brokers and professionals have signed up to get property emailed to them for consideration

Marketedge is a "*power tool*" for reaching the most aggressive and active brokers in the market place. The objective is getting your asset in front of as many active commercial investment professionals as quickly as possible we hope to create an "*auction like atmosphere*" around your property.

That way we can hold the line on price, but more importantly we can hold the line on performance, after all anyone can write you a contract for anything but if it fails to close what did it matter?

This is just another example of how we strive to help you obtain the best possible price and terms for your real property.

Thank you for the opportunity to serve you.

COMMERCIAL INVESTMENT
REAL ESTATE ACADEMY

Tuesday, October 23, 2012

Mr. _____

_____

_____

_____

Re: Property Campaign E-Blast

Dear _____,

This week we blasted you property to over 90,000 commercial real estate brokers nationwide using Property Campaign. Property Campaign is an email push service that is strictly "opt-in" meaning all the brokers and professionals have signed up to get property emailed to them for consideration

Property Campaign is a "*power tool*" for reaching the most aggressive and active brokers in the market place. The objective is getting your asset in front of as many active commercial investment professionals as quickly as possible we hope to create an "*auction like atmosphere*" around your property.

That way we can hold the line on price, but more importantly we can hold the line on performance, after all anyone can write you a contract for anything but if it fails to close what did it matter?

This is just another example of how we strive to help you obtain the best possible price and terms for your real property.

Thank you for the opportunity to serve you.

COMMERCIAL INVESTMENT
REAL ESTATE ACADEMY

May 21, 2017

Mr. _____

_____

_____

_____

Re: Commercial Connected posting

Dear _____,

I just wanted to get you a quick note and copy of our most recent posting. This week we placed your property on Commercial Connected. Commercial Connected is a fast rising star in commercial real estate marketing arena with over 110,000 properties for sale or lease on its website and thousands of unique searches each month. Commercial Connected is fast on its way to rivalling industry leader LoopNet for volume and exposure.

"Commercial Connected is a Professional Commercial Real Estate Sales & Leasing platform designed by Commercial Real Estate Professionals for Commercial Real Estate Professionals."

"With thousands of Commercial Real Estate listings updated daily by top brokerages & owners, Commercial Connected is truly the fastest growing CRE Platform in the country."

Commercial Connected is just another one of the tools that we use to keep your property on the top of the pile and in front of the most active and likely buyers.

Thank you again for your confidence and commitment.

COMMERCIAL INVESTMENT
REAL ESTATE ACADEMY

Monday, October 29, 2012

Mr. _____

_____

_____

Re: LoopNet Listing Status Report

Dear _____,

Enclosed you will please find a copy of our most recent LoopNet Listing Activity Report *"LoopNet is the most heavily trafficked commercial real estate website, with more than 3 million average monthly unique visitors."*

Most investors and buyers of commercial real estate turn to LoopNet to do a preliminary search for potential properties and as such LoopNet is the first line of *"offense"* in promoting your property.

LoopNet also offer a service called property matching, where buyer enter a series of preferences and when a new property is placed on LoopNet the prospective buyer is automatically emailed the new offering. In addition to the property matching service we have the ability to send direct emails to potential interested parties.

As you can see we will leave no stone unturned in our efforts to find you the buyer who will offer the best possible price and terms.

COMMERCIAL INVESTMENT
REAL ESTATE ACADEMY

Sunday, May 21, 2017

Mr. _____

_____

_____

_____

Re: LoopNet Premium E-Mail Prospect List

Dear _____ ,

Enclosed you will please find a copy of our most recent LoopNet advertising, LoopNet *"is the most heavily trafficked commercial real estate website, with more than 3 million average monthly unique visitors."*

Most investors and buyers of commercial real estate turn to LoopNet to do a preliminary search for potential properties and as such LoopNet is the first line of *"offense"* in promoting your property.

LoopNet also offer a service called property matching, where buyer enter a series of preferences and when a new property is placed on LoopNet the prospective buyer is automatically emailed the new offering. In addition to the property matching service we have the ability to send direct emails to potential interested parties.

As you can see we will leave no stone unturned in our efforts to find you the buyer who will offer the best possible price and terms.

COMMERCIAL INVESTMENT
REAL ESTATE ACADEMY

Sunday, May 21, 2017

_____
_____
_____

Re: Realtors Association Greater Fort Lauderdale monthly networking meeting

_____,

This past Friday the Realtors Association of Greater Fort Lauderdale (RAGFLA) had its monthly commercial marketing meeting at the Association office located at 1765 NE 26th St, Fort Lauderdale, FL 33305.

Usually there are 20-40 of the most active commercial real estate professionals in attendance. It is not unusual for one or more of these brokers to have a seller that is looking to either change product type or is looking for a "*replacement property*" for a 1031 tax deferred exchange.

This is just another example of how we endeavor to generate the maximum exposure for your asset and find truly qualified and motivated buyers.

It is not at all uncommon for us to get a call or two regarding a property presented at that meeting in the next few days following the presentation. And as always we will keep you fully informed if any interest is generated from the presentation.

Thank you for your ongoing confidence and commitment.

COMMERCIAL INVESTMENT
REAL ESTATE ACADEMY

Sunday, May 21, 2017

Mr. _____

_____

_____

Re: CCIM Mailbridge broadcast email

_____,

Attached you will please find a copy of a CCIM Mailbridge broadcast email that was sent regarding your property this week. This broadcast went to 13,299 subscribers, 62 weekly subscribers looking specifically for your type of property, 213 subscribers via RSS feed, and 140 that signed up for "real time" alerts.

A CCIM or Certified Commercial Investment Member is a real estate professional that has taken several graduate level courses in commercial real estate, finance, leasing, and sales strategies. Further, a CCIM has demonstrated their competency in commercial real estate by documenting multiple millions of dollars in closed transaction.

There are an estimated 2,000,000 licensed real estate agents in the United States alone there are 16,000 total Designees and Candidates around the world representing the top 6% of all real estate professionals.

This means that when a CCIM has a prospect, that prospect is qualified, has the ability to close a transaction, and will be given expert guidance when pursuing your property. This is just another example of how we strive to keep your property in front of the most probable buyers possible.

Thank you again for the opportunity to serve.

COMMERCIAL INVESTMENT
REAL ESTATE ACADEMY

Sunday, May 21, 2017

Mr. _____

_____

_____

_____

Re: Price Adjustment

Dear _____,

This letter shall serve to confirm our conversation of today's date, wherein we discussed making a price adjustment from the current list price of (Property Address) from (Former Price) to (New Price)

If this confirms your understanding of our conversation, please so indicate by authorizing below and returning a copy of same to my office via facsimile at XXX-XXX-XXXX or email to _____.

Thank you for the opportunity to serve you.

Agreed to and accepted by;

_____
Signature

_____
Print Name

_____
Date

COMMERCIAL INVESTMENT
REAL ESTATE ACADEMY

Sunday, May 21, 2017

Mr. _____

_____

_____

Re: Registration of prospective purchaser

Dear _____,

Below you will please find the name(s) of a "*prospect*" that has expressed an interest in your property as a result of our advertising or promotional campaign.

1. _____
2. _____
3. _____

We have provided them a complete marketing package for their review and consideration. Typically, we will give the prospect a day or two to review and digest the information before we follow up with a telephone call to gauge their level of interest.

It also gives us an opportunity to further qualify them as to their operational experience, financial wherewithal, and overall credibility. We will keep you informed with further bulletins as events warrant.

Thank you for the opportunity to serve you.

COMMERCIAL INVESTMENT
REAL ESTATE ACADEMY

May 21, 2017

Mr. _____

_____

_____

_____

Re: *CommercialSearch.com* posting

Dear _____,

I just wanted to get you a quick note and copy of our most recent posting. This week we placed your property on *CommercialSearch*. *CommercialSearch* is a fast rising star in commercial real estate marketing arena with over 110,000 properties for sale or lease on its website and thousands of unique searches each month. Commercial Connected is fast on its way to rivalling industry leader LoopNet for volume and exposure.

"CommercialSearch was built in collaboration with the industry to offer a better commercial real estate marketplace alternative. It's free, easy to use and packed with features. It's embraced by the world's largest firms so the content is great. It's endorsed by NAR and Realtor.com so your marketing reach is unparalleled. And it's created by Xceligent who has built its business by partnering with the community and people like you."

CommercialSearch is just another one of the tools that we use to keep your property on the top of the pile and in front of the most active and likely buyers.

Thank you again for your confidence and commitment.

COMMERCIAL INVESTMENT
REAL ESTATE ACADEMY

May 21, 2017

Mr. _____

_____

_____

_____

Re: CommercialSearch.com posting

Dear _____,

I just wanted to get you a quick note and copy of our most recent posting. This week we placed your property on CommercialSearch.com. CommercialSearch.com is a fast rising star in commercial real estate marketing arena with over 450,000 properties for sale or lease on its website and over 2 million unique searches each month. CommercialSearch.com is fast on its way to rivalling industry leader LoopNet for volume and exposure.

CommercialSearch.com has over 258,385 user accounts from over 36,000 different companies. CommercialSearch.com is in 40 markets across the country.

CommercialScarch.com is just another one of the tools that we use to keep your property on the top of the pile and in front of the most active and likely buyers.

Thank you again for your confidence and commitment.

COMMERCIAL INVESTMENT
REAL ESTATE ACADEMY

Sunday, May 21, 2017

Mr. _____

_____

_____

_____

Re: Crittenden Real Estate Investors Directory

Dear _____,

This week we combed the *Crittenden Real Estate Investors Directory* for likely prospects for your property. The Crittenden Real Estate Investors Directory is described as follows;

" The Real Estate Investors directory details buying criteria for over 500 companies including public and nontraded REITs, foreign investors, institutional investors, pension funds and fast-growing regional buyers."

"For more than 40 years, Crittenden's real estate directories and reports have offered an insider's view into the plans of lenders, developers, retail tenants and real estate buyers. An editorial staff with years of experience delivers insightful and relevant information on the who, what, where, how and why."

As you can imagine, not all 500 are viable candidates for your property however we identified those that have an interest in your property type, in your property's market area and initiated contact via email. We have gotten some responses and will be following up on those inquiries.

As always...*"further bulletins as events warrant!"*

COMMERCIAL INVESTMENT
REAL ESTATE ACADEMY

Sunday, May 21, 2017

Mr. _____

_____

_____

Re: Broward CCIM Districts Monthly Commercial meeting.

Dear _____,

This Wednesday the Broward CCIM District had its monthly commercial marketing meeting at the The Signature Grand Convention, in Davie Florida.

Usually there are 40-60 of the most active CCIM's in the marketplace in attendance. It is not unusual for one or more of these brokers to have a seller that is looking to either change product type or is looking for a *"replacement property"* for a 1031 tax deferred exchange.

This is just another example of how we endeavor to generate the maximum exposure for your asset and find truly qualified and motivated buyers.

It is not at all uncommon for us to get a call or two regarding a property presented at that meeting in the next few days following the presentation. And as always we will keep you fully informed if any interest is generated from the presentation.

Thank you for your ongoing confidence and commitment.

COMMERCIAL INVESTMENT
REAL ESTATE ACADEMY

Sunday, May 21, 2017

Mr. _____

_____

_____

Re: (Franchise) Commercial website

Dear _____,

Enclosed you will please find a copy of our most recent (FRANCHISE) Commercial Website advertising. The (FRANCHISE) System is comprised of approximately 7,000 independently owned and operated franchised broker offices and 110,000 agents in 79 countries and territories worldwide.

The (FRANCHISE) Commercial System is comprised of commercial real estate professionals serving clients around the globe. As leaders in their respective markets, (FRANCHISE) Commercial professionals offer unparalleled local insight, helping you make informed decisions that enhance value across geographic and cultural boundaries.

As you can see we will leave no stone unturned in our efforts to find you the buyer who will offer the best possible price and terms.

Friday, May 20, 2016

Mr. _____

_____

_____

_____

Re: *XYZ Realty* mailing

Dear Scott,

Attached you will please find a copy of a *XYZ Realty* email that was sent regarding your property this week.

XYZ Realty has been a local market leader in commercial real estate sales, leasing and management for over 60 years combined experience. *XYZ Realty* is known for its total commitment to meeting or exceeding our clients' needs and expectations in any commercial real estate transaction.

As part of our ongoing commitment to you we have emailed your property flyer (enclosed) to our data base of over 600 commercial brokers, owners, and managers in South Florida. This is just one of the many ways we try to keep your property at the "head of the line" in potential buyer's minds.

Thank you again for the opportunity to serve.

Sunday, May 21, 2017

Mr. _____

_____

_____

Attached you will please find a copy of a *XYZ Realty* email that was sent regarding your property this week.

XYZ Realty has been a local market leader in commercial real estate sales, leasing and management for over 60 years combined experience. *XYZ Realty* is known for its total commitment to meeting or exceeding our clients' needs and expectations in any commercial real estate transaction.

As part of our ongoing commitment to you we have emailed your property flyer (enclosed) to our data base of over 600 commercial brokers, owners, and managers in South Florida. This is just one of the many ways we try to keep your property at the "head of the line" in potential buyer's minds.

Thank you again for the opportunity to serve.

COMMERCIAL INVESTMENT
REAL ESTATE ACADEMY

Sunday, May 21, 2017

Mr. _____

_____

_____

_____

Re: CREXi Listing Promotion

Dear _____,

Enclosed you will please find a copy of our most recent CREXi advertising, Exceligent *"CREXi is a commercial real estate marketplace that simplifies transactions for brokers with a suite of easy-to-use tools to manage the entire process from listing to closing. Bringing the traditional CRE sales process online, CREXi leverages the latest advances in technology to make transactions ultra efficient.."*

CREXi's central focus, as a revolutionary marketplace and venue for commercial real estate sales, marketing and promotion, is to ensure that all Sellers have a seamless and unparalleled client experience, which is why CREXi only conducts Sales Events on behalf of Sellers.

In addition to general information, a Property Page may also provide interested buyers with purchase guidelines, photographs and related media, title histories, current rent rolls, environmental and technical reports, and other pertinent information relating to the valuation and/or earning potential of an Asset.

CREXi, backed by a diverse group of investors including freestyle.vc, LHV, FOUNDER Collective, TenOneTen, Leon Capital Group and Karlin Ventures and is one of the fastest growing commercial real estate platforms in the market.

As you can see we will leave no stone unturned in our efforts to find you the buyer who will offer the best possible price and terms.

COMMERCIAL INVESTMENT
REAL ESTATE ACADEMY

Sunday, May 21, 2017

Mr. _____

_____

_____

Re: Expresscopy postcard campaign

Dear _____,

In the never ending "*quest*" to expose your property to the widest possible target audience. We have identified a group of owners and investors in the market area that have expressed an interest in your type of property.

To that end we have produced the attached postcard and sent it to those "*suspects*" that we feel would be the most likely to purchase/lease your property. We have also "*seeded*" the list so we can be assured of the date of delivery.

As always, our objective is to put buyers in a "*controlled competition*" for your asset, that way we not only hold the line on price but more importantly on performance. From time to time we will be providing you copies of promotional materials, registrations, and the names of parties that have inquired so you know exactly what we are doing on your behalf.

Thank you again for the opportunity to serve.

COMMERCIAL INVESTMENT
REAL ESTATE ACADEMY

Monday, October 29, 2012

Mr. _____

_____

_____

Re: Realtors Association of Miami and the Beaches Commercial Market Place

Dear _____,

This Thursday the Realtors Association of Miami and the Beaches (RAMB) had its monthly commercial marketing meeting at the Association office located at 700 Poinciana Boulevard, Suite 400, Miami.

Usually there are 40-60 of the most active commercial real estate professionals in attendance. It is not unusual for one or more of these brokers to have a seller that is looking to either change product type or is looking for a *"replacement property"* for a 1031 tax deferred exchange.

This is just another example of how we endeavor to generate the maximum exposure for your asset and find truly qualified and motivated buyers.

It is not at all uncommon for us to get a call or two regarding a property presented at that meeting in the next few days following the presentation. And as always we will keep you fully informed if any interest is generated from the presentation.

Thank you for your ongoing confidence and commitment.

COMMERCIAL INVESTMENT
REAL ESTATE ACADEMY

July 24, 2014

Mr. _____

_____

_____

_____

Re: ICI World Listing Posting

Dear _____,

Attached you will please find a copy of an ICI World advertisement posting on your property. ICI World is one of the earliest global real estate "Haves and Wants" databases of real estate operating since 1994 and the first to include mobile device application.

It is a free to search information data base for everyone, the public, buyers, sellers, developers, Pension Funds, Reits, and all who are interested in buying, selling and leasing of real estate. ICI World has a strong market following in Canadian professionals and professional from the United States and is accessed globally. This data base includes residential real estate, business opportunities, and all commercial properties types.

Thank you again for the opportunity to serve.

COMMERCIAL INVESTMENT
REAL ESTATE ACADEMY

Sunday, May 21, 2017

Mr./Mrs. _____
_____
_____

Re: Submission to leading lenders

Dear _____,

One of the most critical parts to a commercial investment real estate transaction is financing. In fact the National Association of Realtors published a statistic that stated *"97% of all real estate transaction requires some form of financing"*

To that end we have submitted your property to the lenders listed below for preliminary review:

1.
2.
3.

The reason we do that is so that we can identify terms and conditions under which lenders will lend on your property. That way we can *"head 'em off at the pass"* in the event that a potential buyer has a difficult time finding the right lender.

We should have an *"expression of interest"* back from the lenders with a list of terms and conditions that we can include in our marketing materials. This way we can make the process of buying your property quicker and easier for the buyer...and more likely to close quickly and at a higher price for you!

This is just another of the many tools that we use to help maximize your return while minimizing the time and energy it takes to get a transaction closed.

Thank you again for the opportunity to serve you.

COMMERCIAL INVESTMENT
REAL ESTATE ACADEMY

Sunday, May 21, 2017

Mr. _____

_____

_____

_____

Re: Promoting your property on 42Floors

Dear ____,

Enclosed you will please find a copy of our most recent 42Floors advertising post. 42Floors is a National marketplace dedicated solely to marketing spaces for lease across the country. 42Floors is the fastest growing site dedicated to commercial leasing in the market place today. Tenants, brokers, and allied professionals use 42Floors to help identify possible locations quickly and easily.

As of today, 42Floors tracks over 6.3 Billion square feet of available space for lease. There is an average of 27,000 new leasing opportunities entered each month. 42Floors has over 500,000 unique property listings and gets over 200,000 unique visits each month.

In the past 12 months alone 42Floors has added more than 20,000 broker/members in 65 new markets and added over 270,000 new listings.

As you can see we will leave no stone unturned in our efforts to find you the buyer who will offer the best possible price and terms.

COMMERCIAL INVESTMENT
REAL ESTATE ACADEMY

Sunday, May 21, 2017

Mr. _____

_____

_____

Re: Listing Expiration

Dear _____,

This letter shall serve to confirm our conversation of today's date, wherein we discussed that our exclusive marketing agreement regarding the property located at
_____ is scheduled to expire on _____.

We will be sending you a letter registering all the parties that we have introduced to your property during our marketing period we will continue to monitor those prospects during the protection period, however we will cease any marketing activity on your behalf in accordance with your request.

If this confirms your understanding of our conversation, please so indicate by authorizing below and returning a copy of same to my office via facsimile at XXX-XXX-XXXX or email to
_____.

Thank you for the opportunity to serve you.

Agreed to and accepted by;

_____
Signature

_____
Print Name

_____
Date

COMMERCIAL INVESTMENT
REAL ESTATE ACADEMY

Sunday, May 21, 2017

Mr. _____

_____

_____

_____

Re: Listing extension and renewal

Dear _____,

This letter shall serve to modify that certain Single Agent Representation Agreement by and between (Broker) and (Seller), (address) and dated (date).

More fully described as;

_____

It is agreed by and between (Broker) and (Seller) that the listing shall be extended for a period of 180 days from (Date) until (date) unless otherwise terminated by either party all other terms and conditions as set forth in the original agreement shall remain in full force and effect.

If this confirms your understanding of our conversation, please so indicate by authorizing below and returning a copy of same to my office via facsimile at XXX-XXX-XXXX

Thank you again for your consideration.

Agreed to and accepted by;

_____
(Seller)

Date: _____

COMMERCIAL INVESTMENT
REAL ESTATE ACADEMY

Sunday, May 21, 2017

_____
_____
_____

Re: MLS on line marketing site

Dear _____,

I have enclosed for your review for the MLS posting we created for your property. The MLS is a listing service with over 80,000 members in the Tri-county area, 47,000 active listings and is the Largest Real Estate Board in the United States.

Real Estate Professionals use MLS as a way quickly accessing the latest offerings in the commercial market. The site features allied professionals in lending, appraisals, and other services, professionals who often have clients that are looking for new acquisitions.

The MLS is comprised of both commercial and residential brokers throughout the United States, Canada, and the Caribbean. South and Central American brokers and principals have access to the service as well and with the political climate and resurgence of the Brazilian economy it is not at all usual to have foreign capital looking for a home right here in South Florida.

MLS is one of the many ways seek to uncover the most probable, qualified potential buyer for your property.

Thank you again for your business.

COMMERCIAL INVESTMENT
REAL ESTATE ACADEMY

Sunday, May 21, 2017

Mr. _____

_____

_____

Re: NMLS (National Multiple Listing Service) postcard campaign

Dear _____,

In the never ending "*quest*" to expose your property to the widest possible target audience. We have identified a group of owners and investors in the market area that have expressed an interest in your type of property.

To that end we have produced the attached postcard and sent it to those "*suspects*" that we feel would be the most likely to purchase/lease your property. We have also "*seeded*" the list so we can be assured of the date of delivery.

As always, our objective is to put buyers in a "*controlled competition*" for your asset, that way we not only hold the line on price but more importantly on performance. From time to time we will be providing you copies of promotional materials, registrations, and the names of parties that have inquired so you know exactly what we are doing on your behalf.

Thank you again for the opportunity to serve.

COMMERCIAL INVESTMENT
REAL ESTATE ACADEMY

Sunday, May 21, 2017

Mr. _____

_____

_____

_____

Re: *QuantumListing* Promotion

Dear _____,

Enclosed you will please find a copy of our most recent QuantumListing is a brand new challenger to LoopNet, CoStar and a number of other commercial listing services.

The beauty of *QuantumListing* is that it is quick and easy to use and like all start-ups it has a lot of excitement in the brokerage community. What that mean is your property benefits from the "*early adopter*" excitement getting more exposure, faster instead of getting lost in the maelstrom of millions of listings.

QuantumListing's unique platform is designed specifically to be iPhone, iPad, and Android friendly so that mobile users get all the information about your property without all the exercise required by the "big boys"

We will continue to find new and innovative ways to find you the buyer who will offer the best possible price and terms for your property.

Sunday, May 21, 2017

Mr. _____

_____

_____

Re: Vistaprints postcard campaign

Dear _____,

In the never ending *"quest"* to expose your property to the widest possible target audience. We have identified a group of owners and investors in the market area that have expressed an interest in your type of property.

To that end we have produced the attached postcard and sent it to those *"suspects"* that we feel would be the most likely to purchase/lease your property. We have also *"seeded"* the list so we can be assured of the date of delivery.

As always, our objective is to put buyers in a *"controlled competition"* for your asset, that way we not only hold the line on price but more importantly on performance. From time to time we will be providing you copies of promotional materials, registrations, and the names of parties that have inquired so you know exactly what we are doing on your behalf.

Thank you again for the opportunity to serve.

COMMERCIAL INVESTMENT
REAL ESTATE ACADEMY

Sunday, May 21, 2017

Mr. _____

_____

_____

_____

Re: Xceligent Listing Promotion

Dear _____,

Enclosed you will please find a copy of our most recent Xceligent advertising, Exceligent *"Xceligent is a leading provider of verified commercial real estate information across the United States."*

Their professional research team pro-actively collects: a comprehensive inventory of commercial properties, buildings available for lease and sale, tenant information, sales comparables, historical trends on lease rates and building occupancy, market analytics, and demographics.

This information assists real estate professionals, appraisers, owners, investors and developers that make strategic decisions to lease, sell and develop commercial properties.

Xceligent, backed by a new global investor, and has launched an aggressive national expansion that will provide researched information in the 65 largest United States markets.

As you can see we will leave no stone unturned in our efforts to find you the buyer who will offer the best possible price and terms.

COMMERCIAL INVESTMENT
REAL ESTATE ACADEMY

Sunday, May 21, 2017

Mr. _____

_____

_____

Re: Realtors Association of Miami and the Beaches Commercial Market Place (DCOTA)

Dear _____,

This Thursday the Realtors Association of Miami and the Beaches (RAMB) had its monthly commercial marketing meeting at the Association office located at 1815 Griffin Road, Suite104, Dania Florida.

Usually there are 40-60 of the most active commercial real estate professionals in attendance. It is not unusual for one or more of these brokers to have a seller that is looking to either change product type or is looking for a "*replacement property*" for a 1031 tax deferred exchange.

This is just another example of how we endeavor to generate the maximum exposure for your asset and find truly qualified and motivated buyers.

It is not at all uncommon for us to get a call or two regarding a property presented at that meeting in the next few days following the presentation. And as always we will keep you fully informed if any interest is generated from the presentation.

Thank you for your ongoing confidence and commitment.

COMMERCIAL INVESTMENT
REAL ESTATE ACADEMY

Sunday, May 21, 2017

Mr. _____

_____

_____

_____

Re: LoopNet advertising and promotion

Gentlemen,

Enclosed you will please find a copy of our most recent LoopNet advertising, LoopNet *"is the most heavily trafficked commercial real estate website, with more than 3 million average monthly unique visitors."*

Most investors and buyers of commercial real estate turn to LoopNet to do a preliminary search for potential properties and as such LoopNet is the first line of *"offense"* in promoting your property.

LoopNet also offer a service called property matching, where buyer enter a series of preferences and when a new property is placed on LoopNet the prospective buyer is automatically emailed the new offering. In addition to the property matching service we have the ability to send direct emails to potential interested parties.

As you can see we will leave no stone unturned in our efforts to find you the buyer who will offer the best possible price and terms.

COMMERCIAL INVESTMENT
REAL ESTATE ACADEMY

Sunday, May 21, 2017

Mr. _____

_____

_____

_____

Re: Total Commercial.com advertising and promotion

Dear _____,

Enclosed you will please find a copy of our most recent Total Commercial.com advertising campaign, Total Commercial is a complete commercial real estate commercial information exchange (CIE) and caters to the commercial real estate community in Florida.

Most investors and buyers of commercial real estate like to invest close to home and Total Commercial gives them a venue to search the Florida market place and keep their investment closer to home.

Total Commercial caters to the entire state of Florida and even powers some of the commercial real estate association website, so it is a go-to power tool for active commercial brokers. Total Commercial boasts a membership of 15,000 with over 250,000 searches each and every week.

Total Commercial is just another "*arrow in our quiver*" in the hunt for the perfect buyer for your real property.

Thank you again for your business.

Sunday, May 21, 2017

Mr. _____

_____

_____

Re: The Brokers List on line marketing sight

Dear _____,

I have enclosed for your review for the Broker List posting we created for your property the Brokers List is an active blog/website that specifically caters to commercial real estate practitioner in Florida.

A great many commercial brokers use the Broker List as a way of finding *"off-market"* as well as on market transaction. The site also has allied professionals in lending, appraisals, and other services, professionals who often have clients that are looking for new acquisitions.

The Broker List is subscribed to by commercial and residential brokers throughout the continental United States and Canada. As you probably already know our market is a prime target for vacationing "snow-birds" and it is not at all uncommon for a visitor to decide to put down roots in our community.

The Brokers List is just another *"tool"* in our marketing tool box that we use to help find the right buyer for your asset.

Thank you again for your business.

Sunday, May 21, 2017

Mr. _____

_____

_____

_____

Re: CIMLS on line marketing site

Dear _____,

I have enclosed for your review for the CIMLS posting we created for your property the CIMLS is a website with over 280,000 members, 400,000 listings, and over $500 Billion in property for sale or lease at any given time.

Commercial brokers use CIMLS as a way quickly accessing the latest offerings in the commercial market. The site features allied professionals in lending, appraisals, and other services, professionals who often have clients that are looking for new acquisitions.

The CIMLS is comprised of both commercial and residential brokers throughout the United States, Canada, and the Caribbean. South and Central American brokers and principals have access to the service as well and with the political climate and resurgence of the Brazilian economy it is not at all usual to have foreign capital looking for a home right here in South Florida.

CIMLS is one of the many ways seek to uncover the most probable, qualified potential buyer for your property.

Thank you again for your business.

COMMERCIAL INVESTMENT
REAL ESTATE ACADEMY

Monday, October 29, 2012

Mr. _____

_____

_____

Re: RealUp on line marketing sight

Dear _____,

Enclosed you will please find a copy of our RealUp posting for your review, RealUp is a commercial real estate website that boast over $150 Billion worth of real estate for sale. RealUp is a free site for Owner/Buyer looking for real property, mortgages, and allied professional services. REalUP has over 100,000 members, and 200,000 property listings.

Tech savvy buyers and users use RealUp a quick and easy to use tool to identify potential buying or leasing opportunities throughout the commercial market place. RealUp features allied professionals in lending, appraisals, and other services, professionals who often have clients that are looking for new acquisitions.

The RealUp is comprised of both commercial and residential brokers throughout the United States, Canada, and the Caribbean. South and Central American brokers and principals have access to the service as well and with the political climate and resurgence of the Brazilian economy it is not at all usual to have foreign capital looking for a home right here in South Florida.

CIMLS is one of the many ways seek to uncover the most probable, qualified potential buyer for your property.

Thank you again for your business.

Commercial Investment Real Estate Academy, LLC ◊ 2893 Executive Park Dr., Suite 303, Weston, FL 33331

COMMERCIAL INVESTMENT
REAL ESTATE ACADEMY

Sunday, May 21, 2017

Mr. _____
_____
_____

Re: Brevitas Listing Promotion

Dear ____,

Enclosed you will please find a copy of our most recent Brevitas listing advertising post. Brevitas is a global marketplace where brokers and buyers can gain access to an exclusive listing inventory. Investors, brokers, and advisors use Brevitas to streamline their investment search while creating long-term relationships in target markets.

As of today, Brevitas has approximately 8240 members and has closed about $421M in transactions. It has an actual inventory of about 1,031 properties at this time.

In addition to general information, a **Property Page** may also provide interested buyers with purchase guidelines, photographs and related media, title histories, current rent rolls, environmental and technical reports, and other pertinent information relating to the valuation and/or earning potential of an Asset. Brevitas attract more buyers with global marketing campaigns targeted to your asset type. It moves faster with automated workflow systems that streamline you transaction process, then track interest in your deal and engage with decision makers who can close.

As you can see we will leave no stone unturned in our efforts to find you the buyer who will offer the best possible price and terms.

COMMERCIAL INVESTMENT
REAL ESTATE ACADEMY

May 21, 2017

Mr. _____

_____

_____

_____

Re: BuzzTarget

Dear _____,

This week we blasted your property to over 90,000 commercial real estate brokers nationwide using BuzzTarget. BuzzTarget is an email push service that is strictly "opt-in" meaning all the brokers and professionals have signed up to get property emailed to them for consideration

BuzzTarget is a "*power tool*" for reaching the most aggressive and active brokers in the market place. The objective is getting your asset in front of as many active commercial investment professionals as quickly as possible we hope to create an "*auction like atmosphere*" around your property.

That way we can hold the line on price, but more importantly we can hold the line on performance, after all anyone can write you a contract for anything but if it fails to close what did it matter?

This is just another example of how we strive to help you obtain the best possible price and terms for your real property.

Thank you for the opportunity to serve you.

COMMERCIAL INVESTMENT
REAL ESTATE ACADEMY

Sunday, May 21, 2017

Mr. _____

_____

_____

_____

Re: CoStar real estate website and broadcast services

Dear _____,

This week we submitted your property to CoStar the Global leader in commercial real estate listing and marketing services. CoStar maintains the largest database of property for sale and lease in the world as you can see below.

"Founded in 1987, CoStar conducts expansive, ongoing research to produce and maintain the largest and most comprehensive database of commercial real estate information. Our suite of online services enables clients to analyze, interpret and gain unmatched insight on commercial property values, market conditions and current availabilities.

Headquartered in Washington, DC, CoStar maintains offices throughout the U.S. and in Europe with a staff of approximately 1,500 worldwide, including the industry's largest professional research organization."

CoStar logs over 5.1 million data changes each day, and logs over 10,000 calls daily to brokers, developers, and other commercial professionals. They currently track 500,000 properties in the US annually and are a go to source for many investors and owners.

Thank you for the ongoing opportunity to continue to serve you.

Sincerely,

Listing Retention Letters

Week	Letter	Date	Date	Date	Date	Date	Date	Date
1	Broker Letter							
2	Salesmanager Letter							
3	MailBridge							
4	Miami RCA							
5	LoopNet							
6	The Brokers List							
7	Total Commercial							
8	CIMLS							
9	RealUp							
10	Catalyst							
11	Backpage							
12	Craigs List							
13	Building Search							
14	FlaCIE							
15	Elistit							
16	E-property Link							
17	Recyber							
18	CoStar							
19	Property Blast							
20	Property Line							
21	Big Boy Blast							
22	Mondinion							
23	Marketedge							
24	Property Campaign							
25	Com. Connected							
26	LoopNet Status							
27	LoopNet Prospects							
28	RAGFLA							
29	Price Adjustment							
30	Quick Registration							
31	Commercial Search							
32	Century 21							
33	CityFeet							
34	Crittenden Buyers							
35	ICI World							
36	Xceligent							
37	Crexi							
38								
39								
40								
41								
42								
43								
44								

Marketing Campaign Checklist

Internet Based Marketing

www.propertyshark.com	☐
www.LoopNet.com	☐
www.cimls.com	☐
www.vast.com	☐
www.backpage.com	☐
www.craigslist.com	☐
www.buildingsearch.com	☐
www.postlets.com	☐
http://www.chooseyouritem.com/realestat	☐
www.elistit.com	☐
www.propbot.com	☐
www.mondinion.com	☐
www.iciworld.com	☐
www.real-buzz.com	☐
www.recybernetwork.com	☐
www.totalcommercial.com	☐
www.propertyline.com	☐
www.thebrokerslist.com	☐
http://pd.stdb.com/login.aspx	☐
http://realestate.oodle.com/	☐
www.realestatedealsheet.com	☐
www.activerain.com	☐
www.cityfeet.com	☐
www.costar.com	☐
www.sibdu.com	☐
www.usbiztrader.com	☐
www.42floors.com	☐
www.commercialconnected.com	☐
www.commercialsearch.com	☐
www.officespace.com	☐

Social Media

Twitter	☐
Facebook	☐
Linkedin	☐
Plurk	☐
Plaxo Pulse	☐
Ping.fm	☐
Wordpress	☐
Flickr	☐
Myspace	☐
G Talk Status	☐

Linkedin & Yahoo Groups

Personal Contacts/Meetings

Sales Meeting Presentation	☐
RAMB-Breakfast Meeting	☐
RAGFLA-Breakfast Meeting	☐
CCIM Mailbridge	☐

Adam P. Von Romer, CCIM

2893 Executive Park Drive, Suite 304 Weston FL 33331
954-495-1818
info@adamvonromer.com
www.adamvonromer.com

Brief Biography;

Adam P. Von Romer, CCIM has been in real estate 33 years. Adam is an Author, Speaker, Seminar Leader, Real Estate Instructor, and Licensed Real Estate Broker.

Mr. Von Romer has been licensed in both Pennsylvania and Florida and current holds a valid active Broker Associates License with the KoRes Corp. Mr. Von Romer has been a Real Estate Instructor, Mortgage Broker, Mortgage Brokerage Instructor, Community Association Manager, and Community Association Manager Instructor.

Mr. Von Romer has the number one best-selling book on Amazon in the commercial real estate field titled "Getting Started In Commercial Real Estate" ... http://amzn.to/1uGAOfe Mr. Von Romer has taught thousands of students how to make the transition from selling residential real estate to being successful in commercial investment real estate sales and leasing.

Mr. Von Romer has personally closed, managed, or supervised in excess of $1.6 Billion in commercial transaction. Recently he has closed on an industrial property ($2,995,000) that had been on the market with other firms for five years. He has closed recently two Walgreens one valued at $6.8 Million and one valued at $4.85 million.

Mr. Von Romer has been awarded the CCIM designation, CCIM or Certified Commercial Investment Member is a designation awarded by the Commercial Investment Real Estate Institute a division of the National Association of Realtors. The designation has been likened to the Ph. D. of commercial real estate last year CCIM's closed over $200 Billion in transaction.

A complete resume, references are all available upon request.